THE *Fashion* QUESTIONNAIRE

Rosalynde Van

© 2008 Assouline Publishing
601 West 26th Street, 18th floor
New York, NY 10001, USA
Tel.: 212 989-6810 Fax: 212 647-0005
www.assouline.com

Page 5, 6 & 10: © François Berthoud
Page 15 & 94: © Gladys Perint Palmer

Color separation by Luc Alexis Chasleries
Printed in China
Translated questionnaires from the French by Nancy Dunham

ISBN (Black cover): 978 275940 2717
ISBN (White cover): 978 275940 2731

Introduction by Michael Specter

THE Fashion QUESTIONNAIRE

ASSOULINE

Introduction
by Michael Specter

Fashion is an elusive concept, hard to define yet impossible to ignore. For centuries, many people have wished to trivialize fashion's importance; however, the way we present ourselves to the world matters, and it always has. Polonius may be Shakespeare's definitive windbag, but his platitudes wouldn't be memorable if they weren't also true. "Apparel oft proclaims the man," he tells his only son Laertes, before he sets out for France. That fact—and it is a fact—annoyed intellectuals in Shakespeare's day, and it annoys intellectuals now. Nietzsche raged against the "absurd" practice of ceding to influential and powerful people the ability to impose, with tyrannical certainty, their values on others. "The judgment of their taste and nausea," he called it. But, really, who was he kidding?

The most conventional way to look at history is to figure out who won which war; perhaps it would make more sense to focus on who was wearing what and when. Wars are the result of politics, momentous struggles for power; fashion is by definition changeable and inconstant. What matters urgently this week in fashion may soon mean nothing. Fashion presents a snapshot, but it is a snapshot of the collective expression of an era's social and emotional desires. One can learn as much about the values of Neolithic cavemen by examining their loincloths and leggings as by studying their Stone-Age tools.

Often, it matters not so much what people wore but why they wore it. People use the way they look to announce who they are and who they want to be; they proclaim their rank in society, their goals, their attitudes, and their desires, whether personal, professional, and above all, sexual. The way one dresses, the sense of style he or she conveys, might as well be a dog whistle: If that particular frequency reaches you, then the message makes sense. If not, it might as well be in a language you can't speak (or even hear). Nor has there ever been a language with more tenses, clauses, and nuance. In Europe, for years a lady owned clothing that was meant to be worn before noon (Negligee, for instance, means something to be worn negligently, or in a careless, easy manner.) Nobody would have confused the "morning walking dress" with the slightly more elaborate "promenade dress," and neither could be mistaken for an extravagantly trimmed and highly coveted ball gown. Of course, a lady didn't buy these dresses—she had them made. The idea of two women showing up at a dinner in the same dress, coat, or pair of shoes would have made no more sense to them than had each given birth to the same child.

Concerning twentieth-century European history, no one has ever displayed a more highly calibrated understanding of the relationship between social position and fashion than Marcel Proust, who, among his other notable literary achievements, was perhaps the most eminent society columnist of his time. In *Swann's Way*, he described fashion as something that "emanates from a comparatively small number of leaders, who project it . . . over the widening circle of their friends and the friends of their friends, whose names form a sort of tabulated index. People 'in society' know this index by heart, they are gifted in such matters with an erudition from which they have extracted a sort of taste, of tact, so automatic in its operation that Swann, for example, without needing to draw upon his knowledge of the world, if he read in a newspaper the names of the people who had been guests at a dinner, could tell at once how fashionable the dinner had been, just as a man of letters, merely by reading a phrase, can estimate exactly the literary merit of its author."

High-society was set apart—by name and by fashion. Shopgirls never had the "luxury" of getting trussed up in a corset, nor would a chimney sweep have had much use for an Edwardian gentleman's fine white gloves (let alone the means to buy a pair). It may be true that no man is a hero to his valet, but it was certainly true—for two centuries or more—that no man of substance would live without one. Oddly enough, the higher a woman ranked in society, the more likely she was to have been burdened with clothing that made it nearly impossible for her to move about on her own; clothing was about restriction. A woman hemmed in by bustles, swathed in acres of petticoats, and teetering on impossibly high heels was most certainly not a laborer. Clothes such as these were more than fussy; one needed help to put them on and take them off. Dependence was the point, and nothing has made that more obvious than the history of footwear. For a thousand years, the deformed appendages that were Chinese women's feet were seen as intensely erotic, but they were also a sign of status. The idea was clear enough: A woman who can't walk doesn't need to walk. But, a peasant has other uses for her feet. The practice of foot-binding was banned in 1912. In the West, simple, comfortable shoes had emerged around the time of the French Revolution, to accompany the burgeoning idea of equality.

Equality, however desirable as a goal for humanity, has never been fashionable. Alluring and equal don't add up. But if the sewing machine and the Industrial Revolution, and the invention of new fibers and threads that came with them, all had permanent and profound effects on fashion, so did a world in which leisure was no longer simply for the rich. Yet it wasn't until the new technologies crashed into World War I that fashion changed fundamentally. Women suddenly mattered in ways they never had before, toiling furiously to make the planes and bombs and ships their men needed to wage war. It was a liberation of sorts, and millions joining the work-force needed clothing they could wear on the factory floor. Ready-to-wear clothing not only became possible but essential: Crinolines and cumbersome pleats were fine for that rarified elite who never needed to venture much farther than their drawing rooms—but the modern world demanded new fabrics and an easy way to wear them. Women began dressing more casually—even wearing, for the first time, pants and uniforms that in many ways mimicked those worn by the men who were on the front lines. (It is not a trend that has entirely vanished, as any trip to Capitol Hill or the executive suite of a major bank would demonstrate).

But fashion has never fully been about utility. The realms of fantasy and glamour and sex always overlap with clothes. Certainly nothing made that case more clearly than Christian Dior's New Look in the 1940s. His opulently made, romantic dresses showcased rounded shoulders and tightly cinched waists. The pieces seemed somehow outlandish to many people in a country that had just emerged from the deprivations of the Second World War. Glamour had its day, though. "Dior has done for Paris couture what the taxi drivers did for France at the Battle of the Marne," one fashion writer said at the time, referencing the fleet of cabbies who ferried reservists to the front line during World War I. It wasn't hard to peek behind the curtain and see what was happening. When the war ended, men needed their jobs back. So women, swaddled and wrapped like packages, were eased safely back onto their pedestals.

Keeping them there has not been easy. The history of the last century is the history of a world made smaller and more democratic. Movies played a big role in changing attitudes and clothing. Nearly anybody could afford to see a film, and by the 1950s, women in America begin to devour the fashions they saw in movies such as Federico Fellini's *La Dolce Vita*. Life on the Via Veneto seemed casual and carefree, and women began to dress accordingly. When Audrey Hepburn appeared in *Breakfast at Tiffany's* wearing ballet pumps, oversize sunglasses, and a trench coat—an ensemble that even today looks stylish and fresh—it marked the first time a fashion designer, Hubert de Givenchy, worked with an actress to establish the "look" of a film. Suddenly, taste had new arbiters—not Proust or Jean Cocteau, but Hepburn (both Audrey and Katharine) and Lauren Bacall. Fashion is parasitic; it needs to affix itself to a trend, to live off a time or a place. With Hollywood leading the way, the ageless flow of culture from Europe to America reversed almost overnight. How could it have been any other way? The twentieth century was, after all, the "American Century." If James Dean put on a pair of Levis and a T-shirt, so did half the Left Bank of Paris.

It is not yet clear in whose century we now reside. The borders of taste keep expanding as the globe gets smaller. People may, if they wish, still shop directly from the pages of *Vogue* (whether the American, British, French, Indian, Russian, or other international editions), and many women do. But on the street, it is not at all unusual to see a well dressed woman wearing a three thousand dollar sweater draped carelessly over a strategically ripped pair of jeans. Style is as likely to rise from the ground as to fall from the heavens. "I have often said that I wish I had invented blue jeans," Yves Saint Laurent once wrote. "The most spectacular, the most practical, the most relaxed and nonchalant. They have expression, modesty, sex appeal, simplicity—all I hope for in my clothes." Surely, Dior would have fainted. But fashion has never reached more people or been more relevant than it is today. What Karl Lagerfeld or John Galliano put on the runway on a Sunday is seen by a billion people within the week (and often by millions live on the Internet). The clothes are copied and the knockoffs are often sold on the streets of Paris before they appear in a designer's own shop. It may be unfortunate, but what these creators have to say about issues such as global warming, animal rights, politics, is followed as closely by many people as the utterances of Nobel Prize winners. For better or worse, celebrity and fashion have fused. People may be able to shop online and wear what they like, but they are no less eager to learn that Oscar de la Renta's favorite fabric is silk or to know which film most inspires Valentino (George Cukor's *The Women*).

The power of fashion often mystifies even the people who are responsible for it, but then it always has. "Everyone who is smart says they hate fashion, that it's such a waste of time," Miuccia Prada said not long ago. "I have asked many super serious people, 'Then why is fashion so popular?' Nobody can answer that question. But somebody must be interested, because when I go to the stores the people are there. Thousands of them."

They answered...

THOM BROWNE.

Thom Browne

Your symbol of high fashion. PROVOCATION .

Your favourite fabric. WOOL .

Your favourite colour. GREY .

The collection you will never forget. THE LAST ONE .

The style you most dislike. THE LATEST STYLE .

Your favourite fashion photographer. RICHARD AVEDON .

Your favourite model. ~

Your shoe/shoe designer fetish. CLASSIC AMERICAN WING TIPS .

Your jewel/jewelry designer fetish. ~

Your favourite fashion accessory. TIE AND TIE BAR .

Your ideal bag. OLD SAMSONITE BRIEFCASE .

The most creative designer. THERE ARE SO MANY .

The most timeless designer. COCO CHANEL .

Your favourite designer. I DON'T HAVE A FAVORITE .

Your favourite decade in fashion. 1955 - 1965 .

Your contemporary muse or inspiration. REAL PEOPLE .

Your historical muse or icon. REAL PEOPLE .

The "look" you prefer for a man. SUIT WITH WHITE SHIRT AND TIE .

The "look" you prefer for a woman. CLASSIC YET INDIVIDUAL .

The fashion faux pas you can tolerate most. TAKING A CHANGE .

The fashion faux pas you can tolerate least. NOT TAKING A CHANCE .

What is your present state of mind? HAPPY .

Your fashion motto. ALWAYS STRIVE TO BE TRUE TO YOURSELF .

Ennio Capasa

Your symbol of high fashion. SILF

Your favourite fabric. SATIN

Your favourite colour. RED

The collection you will never forget. THE FIRST WOMEN COLLECTION I SHOWED IN OCTOBER 1986

The style you most dislike. SHOW OFF

Your favourite fashion photographer. SAM HASKINS

Your favourite model. KATE MOSS

Your shoe/shoe designer fetish. SATIN SANDALS

Your jewel/jewelry designer fetish. DIAMONDS

Your favourite fashion accessory. SHOES

Your ideal bag. ACCROSS THE BODY IN THE SOFTEST LEATHER

The most creative designer. REI KANAKUBO

The most timeless designer. MYSELF

Your favourite designer. MADAME CHANEL

Your favourite decade in fashion. '65 - '75

Your contemporary muse or inspiration. MY WIFE

Your historical muse or icon. CHARLOTTE RAMPLING

The "look" you prefer for a man. BLACK JEANS, WHITE SHIRT, BLACK WAISTCOAT AND A LOOSE PIECE OK FABRIC AROUND THE NECK

The "look" you prefer for a woman. SLIM PANTS, TAYLORED JACKET

The fashion faux pas you can tolerate most. BEING TOO TRENDY

The fashion faux pas you can tolerate least. TO WEAR MORE THAN THREE COLOURS AT THE SAME TIME

What is your present state of mind? ENTHUSIASTIC

Your fashion motto. FASHION CHANGES EVERYDAY. FASHION NEVER CHANGES

21

Pierre Cardin

Your symbol of high fashion. A laboratory of ideas.

Your favourite fabric. Wool.

Your favourite colour. Green.

The collection you'll never forget. My Cosmos line from 1968.

The style you most dislike. Neglected style.

Your favourite fashion photographer. No one in particular.

Your favourite model. Maryse.

Your shoe/shoe designer fetish. Boots.

Your jewel/jewelry designer fetish.

Your favourite fashion accessory. Towels.

Your ideal bag.

The most creative designer. Paco Rabanne.

The most timeless designer.

Your favourite designer. Courrèges.

Your favourite decade in fashion. The 1970s.

Your contemporary must or inspiration. Scientists.

Your historical muse or icon. Albert Camus.

The "look" you prefer for a man. Clothing that fits a function.

The "look" you prefer for a woman. Clothing that fits a function.

The fashion faux pas you can tolerate most. Not respecting protocol.

The fashion faux pas you can tolerate least.

What is your present state of mind? Amazed.

Your fashion motto. Always more.

Jean-Charles Castelbajac

Your symbol of high fashion. Savoir-vivre and Savoir-faire.

Your favourite fabric. Snow.

Your favourite colour. Good manners and knowledge.

The collection you'll never forget. My contemporary art collection.

The style you most dislike. Napoleon III.

Your favourite fashion photographer. Guy Bourdin.

Your favourite model. Helena Christensen.

Your shoe/shoe designer fetish. The "Voyou" by Berluti.

Your jewel/jewelry designer fetish. My father's signet ring.

Your favourite fashion accessory. The chalk holder by Hermès.

Your ideal bag. A Goyard (numbers and colors).

The most creative designer. Stephen Sprouse.

The most timeless designer. André Courrèges.

Your favourite designer.

Your favourite decade in fashion. From 1410 to 1420.

Your contemporary muse or inspiration. My mother, my friends.

Your historical muse or icon. Miyamoto Musashi, Hannibal Barca.

The "look" you prefer for a man. Beautiful shoes, and everything else follows.

The "look" you prefer for a woman. Nothing, natural.

The fashion faux pas you can tolerate most. Fashion.

The fashion faux pas you can tolerate least. Fashion.

What is your present state of mind? Enthusiastic and determined.

Your fashion motto. "A spirited past, a spiritual future."

Roberto Cavalli

Your symbol of high fashion. *the wild sensuality of a snake*

Your favourite fabric. *silk satin*

Your favourite colour. *it's depend on my mood*

The collection you will never forget. *the first one*

The style you most dislike. *volgar kitch*

Your favourite fashion photographer. *Richard Avedon*

Your favourite model. *my wife*

Your shoe/shoe designer fetish. *myself*

Your jewel/jewelry designer fetish. *Suzanne Belperron*

Your favourite fashion accessory. *my cowboy boots*

Your ideal bag. *my pockets*

The most creative designer. *Rei Kawakubo*

The most timeless designer. *Coco Chanel*

Your favourite designer. *Azzedine Alaia*

Your favourite decade in fashion. *the 70's*

Your contemporary muse or inspiration. *femininity*

Your historical muse or icon. *my mother*

The "look" you prefer for a man. *shabby chic*

The "look" you prefer for a woman. *sensual casual*

The fashion faux pas you can tolerate most. *daring for beeing oneself*

The fashion faux pas you can tolerate least. *not daring for being oneself*

What is your present state of mind? *flying ... as always*

Your fashion motto. *a dress can change your life*

Alber Elbaz

Your symbol of high fashion. Individuality.

Your favourite fabric. Destroyed duchess satin and perfect polyester (DD+PP).

Your favourite colour. Black.

The collection you will never forget. "The Bird" collection, my third collection at Lanvin. I felt like a free bird, out of a cage.

The style you most dislike. Fashion victims.

Your favourite fashion photographer. Guy Bourdin.

Your favourite model. Liz Lee at Geoffrey Beene.

Your shoe/shoe designer fetish. Stiletto heels . . . and higher the better!

Your jewel/jewelry designer fetish. JAR.

Your favourite fashion accessory. Optical glasses.

Your ideal bag. Shopping bag.

The most creative designer. Geoffrey Beene.

The most timeless designer. Geoffrey Beene.

Your favourite designer. Geoffrey Beene.

Your favourite decade in fashion. 1920s.

Your contemporary muse or inspiration. Women I know and women I want to know.

Your historical muse or icon. Elizabeth Taylor, forever . . .

The "look" you prefer for a man. Business suit.

The "look" you prefer for a woman. A red dress.

The fashion faux pas you can tolerate most. Plastic surgery.

The fashion faux pas you can tolerate least. Plastic surgery.

What is your present state of mind. Anxious . . . always anxious.

Your fashion motto. Imperfection!

Diane von Furstenberg

Diane von Furstenberg

Your symbol of high fashion. the perfect tuxedo

Your favourite fabric. jersey

Your favourite colour. all colours!

The collection you will never forget. the one I am working on at the moment

The style you most dislike. to pretend to be something you are not

Your favourite fashion photographer. Irving Penn

Your favourite model. Gia

Your shoe/shoe designer fetish. Christian Louboutin

Your jewel/jewelry designer fetish. Jar

Your favourite fashion accessory. my Swiss bracelet

Your ideal bag. a duffle bag

The most creative designer. John Galliano

The most timeless designer. Yves Saint Laurent / Poiret

Your favourite designer. Schiaparelli.

Your favourite decade in fashion. 30's & 70's

Your contemporary muse or inspiration. Angelina Jolie

Your historical muse or icon. Marlene Dietrich — Lee Miller

The "look" you prefer for a man. a good looking intellectual

The "look" you prefer for a woman. a sexy intelligent one

The fashion faux pas you can tolerate most. ignorance

The fashion faux pas you can tolerate least. pretention

What is your present state of mind? serene

Your fashion motto. love is life is love is life

31

John Galliano

Your symbol of high fashion. Haute couture is the Parfum, the undiluted, unrestrained, unapologetic expression. That is the ultimate in craft and creation. Haute couture indulges fantasies and dresses dreams.

Your favourite fabric. The toile—that's where it all begins and the magic happens. The silk, satins, and sheen is all frosting after this stage.

Your favourite colour. The colour caught in sparkling eyes.

The collection you will never forget. My first, my last, my next one—each is as precious as if it were my child.

The style you most dislike. The one that is ashamed, embarrassed, and feels uncomfortable in what it is doing. Dress your soul and let it sing.

Your favourite fashion photographer. How can you name only one? The ones I've worked with and the ones I wish I had!

Your favourite model. The ones that define "Super" and make you feel as if you've been electrified when they enter the room.

Your shoe/shoe designer fetish. The great—and greatest—the Maestro Manolo Blahnik.

Your jewel/jewelry designer fetish. A woman is the greatest jewel of them all, the greatest diamonds lose their sparkle next to a woman in love.

Your favourite fashion accessory. A smile, failing that a Stephen Jones flirtation, is the ultimate crowning glory!

Your ideal bag. The latest! The newest! The most limited edition! Live and carry luxury!

The most creative designer. Bansky, Jasper Morrison (furniture designer) and the work of Fabien Baron for Cappellini.

The most timeless designer. Mr. Dior of course! He was a revolutionary who defined and who is the New Look.

Your favourite decade in fashion. This one—my decade at Dior.

Your contemporary muse or inspiration. The girl on the street, the girls I work with, the women, ladies, muses and molls. I like women with attitude, charisma, ambition and spirit.

Your historical muse or icon. Models that define their era—that are unique and epitomize their time and period. Marie Antoinette, Mona Lisa, Twiggy, Linda, Naomi, Kate, Gisele.

The "look" you prefer for a man. Top hat, white tie, and tails—it's all about "Puttin' on the Ritz."

The "look" you prefer for a woman. Le Smoking is chic but I don't think you can beat a bias cut beauty—it is glamour from another era.

The fashion faux pas you can tolerate most. When it is obvious that they've made loads of effort yet somehow it still all went wrong.

The fashion faux pas you can tolerate least. When no effort has been made.

What is your present state of mind? Curious, eager, excited, and inspired!

Your fashion motto. J'adore—that's major.

Carolina Herrera

Your symbol of high fashion. The extravagance of details

Your favourite fabric. Gazar.

Your favourite colour. All colors except irridescent

The collection you will never forget. 1981. My first collection.

The style you most dislike. Victorian

Your favourite fashion photographer. Horst, Helmut Newton and Bruce Weber.

Your favourite model. Mounia.

Your shoe/shoe designer fetish. Dal Co, Helene Arpel, and of course the great Manolo.

Your jewel/jewelry designer fetish. Fulco Verdura, Madame Belperron, and James Givenchy

Your favourite fashion accessory. My scent my lipstick and a full lenght mirror.

Your ideal bag. Any bag that does not cost a fortune.

The most creative designer. Elsa Schiaparelli and John Galliano.

The most timeless designer. Cristobal Balenciaga

Your favourite designer. Yves Saint Laurent.

Your favourite decade in fashion. The thirties, the most glamorous.

Your contemporary muse or inspiration. become as unique as blue jeans.

Your historical muse or icon. See the above.

The "look" you prefer for a man.

The "look" you prefer for a woman. Chic and glamorous at all times.

The fashion faux pas you can tolerate most. Excess

The fashion faux pas you can tolerate least. Vulgarity.

What is your present state of mind? Unpredictable

Your fashion motto. "The superflous is always such a necessity" - Voltaire.

35

Tommy Hilfiger

Tommy Hilfiger

Your symbol of high fashion. *The creativity of Couture*

Your favourite fabric. *Silk + Cashmere blend*

Your favourite colour. *Navy Blue Always*

The collection you will never forget. *My first in 1985*

The style you most dislike. *"Shoulder pads"*

Your favourite fashion photographer. *Mario Testino is Great*

Your favourite model. *Iman is a classic*

Your shoe/shoe designer fetish. *Louboutin for a Women Lobb for men.*

Your jewel/jewelry designer fetish. *Cartier (1920's)*

Your favourite fashion accessory. *A sense of humor*

Your ideal bag. *I Dont Like Baggage!*

The most creative designer. *Karl Lagerfeld*

The most timeless designer. *Coco Chanel*

Your favourite designer. *Karl Lagerfeld*

Your favourite decade in fashion. *60's for Rock n' Roll inspiration.*

Your contemporary muse or inspiration. *Brad + Angelina for Now.*

Your historical muse or icon. *Grace Kelly - James Dean*

The "look" you prefer for a man. *Simple White Shirt, Jeans, Navy Blazer*

The "look" you prefer for a woman. *Carefree Confidence*

The fashion faux pas you can tolerate most. *I Dont Like Rules*

The fashion faux pas you can tolerate least. *overthinking or overdoing a look*

What is your present state of mind? *Living For Today*

Your fashion motto. *Be confident + Simple is Safe*

37

Donna Karan

Your symbol of high fashion. *Timeless* The Run & Dress was are the Breathless.

Your favourite fabric. Cashmere

Your favourite colour. Black

The collection you will never forget. My first 1984

The style you most dislike. Fashion Victims

Your favourite fashion photographer. .

Your favourite model.

Your shoe/shoe designer fetish. — Boots Comfort Comfort Boots · Ballet Slippers

Your jewel/jewelry designer fetish. — Artist Jewelry Robert Lee Morkers

Your favourite fashion accessory. Scarf, Blanket

Your ideal bag. — Hermes Bach & Pack

The most creative designer. · Comme Des Garçons

The most timeless designer: — Ralph Lauren

Your favourite designer. Yoji Rich Owens

Your favourite decade in fashion. · 50's - 30's Cultures/art 15

Your contemporary muse or inspiration. Nomads —

Your historical muse or icon. Martha Graham —

The "look" you prefer for a man. — Raff - unshaven. Jeans

The "look" you prefer for a woman. one the believes her strength confidence & comfort

The fashion faux pas you can tolerate most. — Victum

The fashion faux pas you can tolerate least.

What is your present state of mind? — URBAN ZEN

Your fashion motto — 7 Easy Pieces Day to Night Sexy & Sensual.

39

Michael Kors

Your symbol of high fashion. RUSSIAN SABLE BATHROBE COAT

Your favourite fabric. CASHMERE

Your favourite colour. CAMEL

The collection you will never forget. FALL 1983 MY 1ST RUNWAY SHOW

The style you most dislike. 1980'S SHOULDER PADDED POWER SUITS

Your favourite fashion photographer. RICHARD AVEDON

Your favourite model. LAUREN HUTTON

Your shoe/shoe designer fetish. FLAT METALLIC CAPRI SANDALS

Your jewel/jewelry designer fetish. SEAMAN SCHEPPS CHAINS

Your favourite fashion accessory. AVIATOR SUNGLASSES

Your ideal bag. CHOCOLATE NAPA CROCODILE CLUTCH

The most creative designer. AZZEDINE ALAIA

The most timeless designer. YVES SAINT LAURENT

Your favourite designer. HALSTON

Your favourite decade in fashion. THE 70'S

Your contemporary muse or inspiration. HERIN LAUPER

Your historical muse or icon. JACKIE ONASSIS

The "look" you prefer for a man. JEANS CASHMERE PULLOVER, NO SOCKS, LOAFERS

The "look" you prefer for a woman. CASHMERE PULLOVER PENCIL SKIRT, BARELEGS & CROC PUMPS

The fashion faux pas you can tolerate most. TOO MUCH JEWELRY

The fashion faux pas you can tolerate least. WEARING SOMETHING STRICTLY BECAUSE ITS A TREND

What is your present state of mind? CONFIDENT & EXCITED

Your fashion motto. THE CONTRADICTION OF SPORTIF & GLAMOUROUS

Karl Lagerfeld

Your symbol of high fashion. Both an artistic and an artisan craft.

Your favourite fabric. White waffle piqué.

Your favourite colour. Black and White. Impossible to state a preference.

The collection you will never forget. I hope it's still to come…

The style you most dislike. The absence of style.

Your favourite fashion photographer. Steichen or Penn.

Your favourite model. Claudia Schiffer, really…

Your shoe/shoe designer fetish. It is fittingly signed "Massaro."

Your jewel/jewelry designer fetish. My heart belongs to Chrome Hearts…

Your favourite fashion accessory. The wide starched collar.

Your ideal bag. For men, there isn't one yet…

The most creative designer. The word [creative] is a bit overused.

The most timeless designer. Design should always be of its time.

Your favourite decade in fashion. The beginning of the twenty-first century suits me fine.

Your contemporary muse or inspiration. My parents. I haven't found any better.

Your historical muse or icon. Louis XIV.

The "look" you prefer for a man. Good manners!

The "look" you prefer for a woman. To have no obligations.

The fashion faux pas you can tolerate most. I'm not a referee and at the same time indulgence isn't my favorite attitude either.

The fashion faux pas you can tolerate least. Grey socks in sandals. There's nothing worse.

What is your present state of mind? Living in the present.

Your fashion motto. Long live the next . . . collection.

Catherine Malandrino

Catherine Malandrino

Your symbol of high fashion. — robe hommage à Picasso YSL

Your favourite fabric. — silk mousseline / organza

Your favourite colour. — ray of light from citrus yellow to amber

The collection you will never forget.
FLAG 2000
HALLELUJAH 2001
URBAN QUEEN 2005
LA COLOMBE 2007

The style you most dislike.

Your favourite fashion photographer. GUY BOURDIN - AVEDON

Your favourite model. Crystèle Saint Louis - Augustin

Your shoe/shoe designer fetish.

Your jewel/jewelry designer fetish. an engagement ring black tahiti pearl + diamond

Your favourite fashion accessory. heels

Your ideal bag. alligator / suitcase

The most creative designer. Yves Saint Laurent

The most timeless designer. Coco

Your favourite designer.

Your favourite decade in fashion. all + the next ones to come

Your contemporary muse or inspiration.

Your historical muse or icon.

The "look" you prefer for a man. Sean Connery in James Bond mix with Peter Fonda in Easy Rider

The "look" you prefer for a woman. Catherine Deneuve do Belle de Jour, Romy Schneider do la piscine

The fashion faux pas you can tolerate most.

The fashion faux pas you can tolerate least.

What is your present state of mind? in love

Your fashion motto. imagine ...

45

Nicole Miller

Your symbol of high fashion. a martini

Your favourite fabric. stretchy crepe not w/ viscose and lycra

Your favourite colour. yellow/green mustard

The collection you will never forget. guy laroche couture show in Paris

The style you most dislike. flats

Your favourite fashion photographer. DAVID LA CHAPELLE

Your favourite model: Jean Shrimpton

Your shoe/shoe designer fetish. Jonathan Kelsey

Your jewel/jewelry designer fetish. virgins, saints + angels

Your favourite fashion accessory. a belt

Your ideal bag. ferragamo

The most creative designer. Jean Paul Gaultier

The most timeless designer. Azzedine Alaia

Your favourite designer. Dries Van Noten

Your favourite decade in fashion. 60's

Your contemporary muse or inspiration. Joss stone

Your historical muse or icon. - the girl from uncle

The "look" you prefer for a man. all in black

The "look" you prefer for a woman. confident

The fashion faux pas you can tolerate most. stirrup pants and pumps

The fashion faux pas you can tolerate least. Big Logos

What is your present state of mind? Laid Back

Your fashion motto. Never Say Never

47

Oscar de la Renta

Your symbol of high fashion. Style

Your favourite fabric. Silk

Your favourite colour. all Happy colors

The collection you will never forget. my first

The style you most dislike. Sloppy

Your favourite fashion photographer. I have many favorites

Your favourite model. all

Your shoe/shoe designer fetish. a Sexy Shoe

Your jewel/jewelry designer fetish. Only real

Your favourite fashion accessory. all those in the last collection

Your ideal bag. Small with big bills inside

The most creative designer.

The most timeless designer. me

Your favourite designer. myself

Your favourite decade in fashion. now

Your contemporary muse or inspiration. a woman with aspirations

Your historical muse or icon. Eve

The "look" you prefer for a man. always a Suit or Sometime

The "look" you prefer for a woman. individuality

The fashion faux pas you can tolerate most. over the Top

The fashion faux pas you can tolerate least. not trying

What is your present state of mind? always looking forward

Your fashion motto. Try for The best !

49

Ralph Rucci

Your symbol of high fashion. A perfectly cut double-faced jacket with its gusset balanced so that the arm moves upward without affecting the sides of the jacket.

Your favourite fabric. Double-faced cashmere

Your favourite colour. Chocolate brown

The collection you will never forget. Halston - Made to Order - Spring 1972 this first showing at the Olympic Tower - all bias... floating panels and flying saucers. He personally cut many of the clothes himself.

The style you most dislike. Anything I dislike has no style to my eye.

Your favourite fashion photographer. Deborah Turbeville.

Your favourite model. Erin O'Connor

Your shoe/shoe designer fetish. Lobb

Your jewel/jewelry designer fetish. Elsa Peretti and JAR

Your favourite fashion accessory. My Cartier Baignoire Watch

Your ideal bag. Hermes Bolide

The most creative designer. Cristobal Balenciaga

The most timeless designer. Mme. Grès

Your favourite designer. Cristobal Balenciaga

Your favourite decade in fashion. High Renaissance

Your contemporary muse or inspiration. Tie - Diana Vreeland & Elsa Peretti

Your historical muse or icon. Pauline de Rothschild

The "look" you prefer for a man. Clean fitted white shirts, smoldering sex

The "look" you prefer for a woman. Grace in movement

The fashion faux pas you can tolerate most. Sneakers

The fashion faux pas you can tolerate least. Small neck scarves fastened with decorative rings

What is your present state of mind? In and out of reality

Your fashion motto. Simple - restraint - God is in the details

51

Sonia Rykiel

Your symbol of high fashion. An instant of pleasure.

Your favourite fabric. Knits.

Your favourite colour. All the blacks.

The collection you will never forget. Silver thimbles that belonged to my Russian grandmother.

The style you most dislike. Style without style.

Your favourite fashion photographer.

Your favourite model. Anne Rohart.

Your shoe/shoe designer fetish. Barefoot.

Your jewel/jewelry designer fetish. All the rings offered by my lovers.

Your favourite fashion accessory. My mother's belt.

Your ideal bag. One with a thousand studded pockets.

The most creative designer. Jean-Paul Gaultier.

The most timeless designer. Jean-Paul Gaultier.

Your favourite designer.

Your favourite decade in fashion.

Your contemporary muse or inspiration. My daughter, my sisters, my friends.

Your historical muse or icon. Lili Brick, Lou Andrea Salome.

The "look" you prefer for a man. Naked with pants.

The "look" you prefer for a woman. Dressed like a man.

The fashion faux pas you can tolerate most. None.

The fashion faux pas you can tolerate least. Too much taste.

What is your present state of mind? Full of fire.

Your fashion motto. Open the doors, I am coming.

Olivier

Olivier Theyskens

Your symbol of high fashion. An expression, a creation or excellence, an exceptional craft and skill.

Your favourite fabric. I love all fabrics.

Your favourite colour. I love all colors passionately.

The collection you will never forget. My first collection, "Gloomy Trips."

The style you most dislike. Dowdiness.

Your favourite fashion photographer. Steven Meisel.

Your favourite model. Kate Moss.

Your shoe/shoe designer fetish. Worn ballet slippers.

Your jewel/jewelry designer fetish. My friend Laetitia Crahay at Chanel.

Your favourite fashion accessory. Some well-chosen jewelry.

Your ideal bag. Mary Poppins' bag.

The most creative designer. Madeleine Vionnet.

The most timeless designer. Coco Chanel.

Your favourite designer.

Your favourite decade in fashion. Post-war and end of the nineteenth century.

Your contemporary muse or inspiration. Difficult to say—there are a lot of people I admire.

Your historical muse or icon. Marilyn Monroe, Michelangelo, Géricault, Jackson Pollock, Alfred Hitchcock, Diana Vreeland.

The "look" you prefer for a man. The suit.

The "look" you prefer for a woman. Anything that can make her more beautiful.

The fashion faux pas you can tolerate most. I am rather tolerant of people who have the bad luck to have poor taste.

The fashion faux pas you can tolerate least. A horrible hairstyle.

What is your present state of mind? Happy, I'm making my own way . . .

Your fashion motto. Let everyone dress (and be) their best.

Isabel Toledo

Your symbol of high fashion. A HIGH FOREHEAD, a noble eyebrow, exquisite body language, and elegant BONES.

Your favourite fabric. 100% NATURAL.

Your favourite colour. IT'S not about COLOR, but its all about TONE for me.

The collection you will never forget. My first own collection in 1985 or 86???—I've forgotten!

The style you most dislike. STYLE without HUMANITY.

Your favourite fashion photographer. I prefer drawings OR anything by BILL CUNNINGHAM.

Your favourite model. DOVIMA, MONA LISA, LEE MILLER.

Your shoe/shoe designer fetish. MANOLO BLAHNIK, because we are both from the CANARY ISLANDS are very hard headed with soft feet.

Your jewel/jewelry designer fetish. ELSA PERETTI.

Your favourite fashion accessory. CLOTHES.

Your ideal bag. A recycled paper bag.

The most creative designer. GOD—she was such an efficient innovator.

The most timeless designer. NATURE.

Your favourite designer. ME.

Your favourite decade in fashion. NOW.

Your contemporary muse or inspiration. ARTIST RUBEN TOLEDO.

Your historical muse or icon. CAVE WOMEN, because they were so resourceful.

The "look" you prefer for a man. NATURALLY GROOMED.

The "look" you prefer for a woman. SMARTLY POLISHED.

The fashion faux pas you can tolerate most. Inappropriate individuality.

The fashion faux pas you can tolerate least. Looking fashionable.

What is your present state of mind? HELPFUL and RECEPTIVE.

Your fashion motto. HAVE A WELL DRESSED MIND.

Valentino

Your symbol of high fashion. The perfection of a dream.

Your favourite fabric. Silk charmeuse.

Your favourite colour. Red.

The collection you will never forget. The last one.

The style you most dislike. Grunge.

Your favourite fashion photographer. Richard Avedon.

Your favourite model. Gisele.

Your shoe/shoe designer fetish.

Your jewel/jewelry designer fetish. Cartier's jewels for Maria Felix.

Your favourite fashion accessory. Shoes.

Your ideal bag. Small.

The most creative designer. Chanel.

The most timeless designer. Me.

Your favourite decade in fashion. The last one.

Your contemporary muse or inspiration. Smart women.

Your historical muse or icon. Marie Antoinette.

The "look" you prefer for a man. A dark suit.

The "look" you prefer for a woman. A mermaid dress.

The fashion faux pas you can tolerate most. Extensions.

The fashion faux pas you can tolerate least. Worn shoes.

What is your present state of mind? Excited to fix the two last collections of my career.

Your fashion motto. Create your own style and avoid changing it at every moment.

The questionnaires. . .

Rosalynde Jan

Your symbol of high fashion. SIMPLE BLACK ELEGANCE

Your favourite fabric. WOOL KNITS, LINEN, COTTON

Your favourite colour. BLACK, BEIGE-CAMEL, COCOA

The collection you will never forget.

The style you most dislike. GRUNGE - TOO LONG PANTS, TOO MUCH CLEAVAGE

Your favourite fashion photographer. AVEDON

Your favourite model. KATE MOSS - CARMEN DELL'OREFICE

Your shoe/shoe designer fetish. MANOLO, CALVIN KLEIN, FERRAGAMO

Your jewel/jewelry designer fetish. WINSTON, MIKIMOTO, GRAFF   DIAMONDS- EMERALDS

Your favourite fashion accessory. SHOES - HANDBAGS

Your ideal bag. LOUIS VUITTON, BRAHMIN, HERMES, CHANEL

The most creative designer. CHANEL, VALENTINO, GIVENCHY, YSL, BALENCIAGA, RALPH LAUREN

The most timeless designer. CHANEL, VALENTINO

Your favourite decade in fashion. 1970'S

Your contemporary muse or inspiration.

Your historical muse or icon. CARMEN DELL'OREFICE

The "look" you prefer for a man. BLACK SILK-WOOL SUIT, WHITE SHIRT, SILK TIE, POLISHED SHOES

The "look" you prefer for a woman. ELEGANT BLACK SIMPLICITY - MINIMAL JEWELRY

The city with the most style. PARIS

Your favourite book or film about fashion. CHANEL - LITTLE BLACK DRESSES

The fashion faux pas you can tolerate most. TRENDS

The fashion faux pas you can tolerate least. TRENDS - JEANS AT DINNER

What is your present state of mind? BEAUTIFUL

Your fashion motto. NO MATTER WHAT YOU WEAR, BEAUTY COMES FROM WITHIN!

SUBSTANCE IS HER STYLE.

For over 60 years the camera has loved
Carmen Dell'Orefice. But her heart belongs to
Boys' Towns of Italy, an international charity
that supports at risk youth. We're proud that
she's helping to make strides in our shoes.

"Wearing the watch all day seems to **improve** my overall **peace of mind and mood.**"

PHILIP STEIN®

Your symbol of high fashion. _____

Your favourite fabric. _____

Your favourite colour. _____

The collection you will never forget. _____

The style you most dislike. _____

Your favourite fashion photographer. _____

Your favourite model. _____

Your shoe/shoe designer fetish. _____

Your jewel/jewelry designer fetish. _____

Your favourite fashion accessory. _____

Your ideal bag. _____

The most creative designer. _____

The most timeless designer. _____

Your favourite decade in fashion. _____

Your contemporary muse or inspiration. _____

Your historical muse or icon. _____

The "look" you prefer for a man. _____

The "look" you prefer for a woman. _____

The city with the most style. _____

Your favourite book or film about fashion. _____

The fashion faux pas you can tolerate most. _____

The fashion faux pas you can tolerate least. _____

What is your present state of mind? _____

Your fashion motto. _____

Your symbol of high fashion. _____

Your favourite fabric. _____

Your favourite colour. _____

The collection you will never forget. _____

The style you most dislike. _____

Your favourite fashion photographer. _____

Your favourite model. _____

Your shoe/shoe designer fetish. _____

Your jewel/jewelry designer fetish. _____

Your favourite fashion accessory. _____

Your ideal bag. _____

The most creative designer. _____

The most timeless designer. _____

Your favourite decade in fashion. _____

Your contemporary muse or inspiration. _____

Your historical muse or icon. _____

The "look" you prefer for a man. _____

The "look" you prefer for a woman. _____

The city with the most style. _____

Your favourite book or film about fashion. _____

The fashion faux pas you can tolerate most. _____

The fashion faux pas you can tolerate least. _____

What is your present state of mind? _____

Your fashion motto. _____

Your symbol of high fashion. _____

Your favourite fabric. _____

Your favourite colour. _____

The collection you will never forget. _____

The style you most dislike. _____

Your favourite fashion photographer. _____

Your favourite model. _____

Your shoe/shoe designer fetish. _____

Your jewel/jewelry designer fetish. _____

Your favourite fashion accessory. _____

Your ideal bag. _____

The most creative designer. _____

The most timeless designer. _____

Your favourite decade in fashion. _____

Your contemporary muse or inspiration. _____

Your historical muse or icon. _____

The "look" you prefer for a man. _____

The "look" you prefer for a woman. _____

The city with the most style. _____

Your favourite book or film about fashion. _____

The fashion faux pas you can tolerate most. _____

The fashion faux pas you can tolerate least. _____

What is your present state of mind? _____

Your fashion motto. _____

Your symbol of high fashion. _____

Your favourite fabric. _____

Your favourite colour. _____

The collection you will never forget. _____

The style you most dislike. _____

Your favourite fashion photographer. _____

Your favourite model. _____

Your shoe/shoe designer fetish: _____

Your jewel/jewelry designer fetish. _____

Your favourite fashion accessory. _____

Your ideal bag. _____

The most creative designer. _____

The most timeless designer. _____

Your favourite decade in fashion. _____

Your contemporary muse or inspiration. _____

Your historical muse or icon. _____

The "look" you prefer for a man. _____

The "look" you prefer for a woman. _____

The city with the most style. _____

Your favourite book or film about fashion. _____

The fashion faux pas you can tolerate most. _____

The fashion faux pas you can tolerate least. _____

What is your present state of mind? _____

Your fashion motto. _____

Your symbol of high fashion. _____

Your favourite fabric. _____

Your favourite colour. _____

The collection you will never forget. _____

The style you most dislike. _____

Your favourite fashion photographer. _____

Your favourite model. _____

Your shoe/shoe designer fetish: _____

Your jewel/jewelry designer fetish. _____

Your favourite fashion accessory. _____

Your ideal bag. _____

The most creative designer. _____

The most timeless designer. _____

Your favourite decade in fashion. _____

Your contemporary muse or inspiration. _____

Your historical muse or icon. _____

The "look" you prefer for a man. _____

The "look" you prefer for a woman. _____

The city with the most style. _____

Your favourite book or film about fashion. _____

The fashion faux pas you can tolerate most. _____

The fashion faux pas you can tolerate least. _____

What is your present state of mind? _____

Your fashion motto. _____

Your symbol of high fashion. _____

Your favourite fabric. _____

Your favourite colour. _____

The collection you will never forget. _____

The style you most dislike. _____

Your favourite fashion photographer. _____

Your favourite model. _____

Your shoe/shoe designer fetish. _____

Your jewel/jewelry designer fetish. _____

Your favourite fashion accessory. _____

Your ideal bag. _____

The most creative designer. _____

The most timeless designer. _____

Your favourite decade in fashion. _____

Your contemporary muse or inspiration. _____

Your historical muse or icon. _____

The "look" you prefer for a man. _____

The "look" you prefer for a woman. _____

The city with the most style. _____

Your favourite book or film about fashion. _____

The fashion faux pas you can tolerate most. _____

The fashion faux pas you can tolerate least. _____

What is your present state of mind? _____

Your fashion motto. _____

Your symbol of high fashion. _____

Your favourite fabric. _____

Your favourite colour. _____

The collection you will never forget. _____

The style you most dislike. _____

Your favourite fashion photographer. _____

Your favourite model. _____

Your shoe/shoe designer fetish. _____

Your jewel/jewelry designer fetish. _____

Your favourite fashion accessory. _____

Your ideal bag. _____

The most creative designer. _____

The most timeless designer. _____

Your favourite decade in fashion. _____

Your contemporary muse or inspiration. _____

Your historical muse or icon. _____

The "look" you prefer for a man. _____

The "look" you prefer for a woman. _____

The city with the most style. _____

Your favourite book or film about fashion. _____

The fashion faux pas you can tolerate most. _____

The fashion faux pas you can tolerate least. _____

What is your present state of mind? _____

Your fashion motto. _____

71

Your symbol of high fashion. _____

Your favourite fabric. _____

Your favourite colour. _____

The collection you will never forget. _____

The style you most dislike. _____

Your favourite fashion photographer. _____

Your favourite model. _____

Your shoe/shoe designer fetish. _____

Your jewel/jewelry designer fetish. _____

Your favourite fashion accessory. _____

Your ideal bag. _____

The most creative designer. _____

The most timeless designer. _____

Your favourite decade in fashion. _____

Your contemporary muse or inspiration. _____

Your historical muse or icon. _____

The "look" you prefer for a man. _____

The "look" you prefer for a woman. _____

The city with the most style. _____

Your favourite book or film about fashion. _____

The fashion faux pas you can tolerate most. _____

The fashion faux pas you can tolerate least. _____

What is your present state of mind? _____

Your fashion motto. _____

Your symbol of high fashion. _____

Your favourite fabric. _____

Your favourite colour. _____

The collection you will never forget. _____

The style you most dislike. _____

Your favourite fashion photographer. _____

Your favourite model. _____

Your shoe/shoe designer fetish. _____

Your jewel/jewelry designer fetish. _____

Your favourite fashion accessory. _____

Your ideal bag. _____

The most creative designer. _____

The most timeless designer. _____

Your favourite decade in fashion. _____

Your contemporary muse or inspiration. _____

Your historical muse or icon. _____

The "look" you prefer for a man. _____

The "look" you prefer for a woman. _____

The city with the most style. _____

Your favourite book or film about fashion. _____

The fashion faux pas you can tolerate most. _____

The fashion faux pas you can tolerate least. _____

What is your present state of mind? _____

Your fashion motto. _____

73

Your symbol of high fashion. _____

Your favourite fabric. _____

Your favourite colour. _____

The collection you will never forget. _____

The style you most dislike. _____

Your favourite fashion photographer. _____

Your favourite model. _____

Your shoe/shoe designer fetish. _____

Your jewel/jewelry designer fetish. _____

Your favourite fashion accessory. _____

Your ideal bag. _____

The most creative designer. _____

The most timeless designer. _____

Your favourite decade in fashion. _____

Your contemporary muse or inspiration. _____

Your historical muse or icon. _____

The "look" you prefer for a man. _____

The "look" you prefer for a woman. _____

The city with the most style. _____

Your favourite book or film about fashion. _____

The fashion faux pas you can tolerate most. _____

The fashion faux pas you can tolerate least. _____

What is your present state of mind? _____

Your fashion motto. _____

Your symbol of high fashion. _____

Your favourite fabric. _____

Your favourite colour. _____

The collection you will never forget. _____

The style you most dislike. _____

Your favourite fashion photographer. _____

Your favourite model. _____

Your shoe/shoe designer fetish. _____

Your jewel/jewelry designer fetish. _____

Your favourite fashion accessory. _____

Your ideal bag. _____

The most creative designer. _____

The most timeless designer. _____

Your favourite decade in fashion. _____

Your contemporary muse or inspiration. _____

Your historical muse or icon. _____

The "look" you prefer for a man. _____

The "look" you prefer for a woman. _____

The city with the most style. _____

Your favourite book or film about fashion. _____

The fashion faux pas you can tolerate most. _____

The fashion faux pas you can tolerate least. _____

What is your present state of mind? _____

Your fashion motto. _____

Your symbol of high fashion. _____

Your favourite fabric. _____

Your favourite colour. _____

The collection you will never forget. _____

The style you most dislike. _____

Your favourite fashion photographer. _____

Your favourite model. _____

Your shoe/shoe designer fetish. _____

Your jewel/jewelry designer fetish. _____

Your favourite fashion accessory. _____

Your ideal bag. _____

The most creative designer. _____

The most timeless designer. _____

Your favourite decade in fashion. _____

Your contemporary muse or inspiration. _____

Your historical muse or icon. _____

The "look" you prefer for a man. _____

The "look" you prefer for a woman. _____

The city with the most style. _____

Your favourite book or film about fashion. _____

The fashion faux pas you can tolerate most. _____

The fashion faux pas you can tolerate least. _____

What is your present state of mind? _____

Your fashion motto. _____

Your symbol of high fashion. _____

Your favourite fabric. _____

Your favourite colour. _____

The collection you will never forget. _____

The style you most dislike. _____

Your favourite fashion photographer. _____

Your favourite model. _____

Your shoe/shoe designer fetish. _____

Your jewel/jewelry designer fetish. _____

Your favourite fashion accessory. _____

Your ideal bag. _____

The most creative designer. _____

The most timeless designer. _____

Your favourite decade in fashion. _____

Your contemporary muse or inspiration. _____

Your historical muse or icon. _____

The "look" you prefer for a man. _____

The "look" you prefer for a woman. _____

The city with the most style. _____

Your favourite book or film about fashion. _____

The fashion faux pas you can tolerate most. _____

The fashion faux pas you can tolerate least. _____

What is your present state of mind? _____

Your fashion motto. _____

Your symbol of high fashion. _____

Your favourite fabric. _____

Your favourite colour. _____

The collection you will never forget. _____

The style you most dislike. _____

Your favourite fashion photographer. _____

Your favourite model. _____

Your shoe/shoe designer fetish. _____

Your jewel/jewelry designer fetish. _____

Your favourite fashion accessory. _____

Your ideal bag. _____

The most creative designer. _____

The most timeless designer. _____

Your favourite decade in fashion. _____

Your contemporary muse or inspiration. _____

Your historical muse or icon. _____

The "look" you prefer for a man. _____

The "look" you prefer for a woman. _____

The city with the most style. _____

Your favourite book or film about fashion. _____

The fashion faux pas you can tolerate most. _____

The fashion faux pas you can tolerate least. _____

What is your present state of mind? _____

Your fashion motto. _____

Your symbol of high fashion. _____

Your favourite fabric. _____

Your favourite colour. _____

The collection you will never forget. _____

The style you most dislike. _____

Your favourite fashion photographer. _____

Your favourite model. _____

Your shoe/shoe designer fetish. _____

Your jewel/jewelry designer fetish. _____

Your favourite fashion accessory. _____

Your ideal bag. _____

The most creative designer. _____

The most timeless designer. _____

Your favourite decade in fashion. _____

Your contemporary muse or inspiration. _____

Your historical muse or icon. _____

The "look" you prefer for a man. _____

The "look" you prefer for a woman. _____

The city with the most style. _____

Your favourite book or film about fashion. _____

The fashion faux pas you can tolerate most. _____

The fashion faux pas you can tolerate least. _____

What is your present state of mind? _____

Your fashion motto. _____

Your symbol of high fashion. _____

Your favourite fabric. _____

Your favourite colour. _____

The collection you will never forget. _____

The style you most dislike. _____

Your favourite fashion photographer. _____

Your favourite model. _____

Your shoe/shoe designer fetish. _____

Your jewel/jewelry designer fetish. _____

Your favourite fashion accessory. _____

Your ideal bag. _____

The most creative designer. _____

The most timeless designer. _____

Your favourite decade in fashion. _____

Your contemporary muse or inspiration. _____

Your historical muse or icon. _____

The "look" you prefer for a man. _____

The "look" you prefer for a woman. _____

The city with the most style. _____

Your favourite book or film about fashion. _____

The fashion faux pas you can tolerate most. _____

The fashion faux pas you can tolerate least. _____

What is your present state of mind? _____

Your fashion motto. _____

Your symbol of high fashion. _____

Your favourite fabric. _____

Your favourite colour. _____

The collection you will never forget. _____

The style you most dislike. _____

Your favourite fashion photographer. _____

Your favourite model. _____

Your shoe/shoe designer fetish. _____

Your jewel/jewelry designer fetish. _____

Your favourite fashion accessory. _____

Your ideal bag. _____

The most creative designer. _____

The most timeless designer. _____

Your favourite decade in fashion. _____

Your contemporary muse or inspiration. _____

Your historical muse or icon. _____

The "look" you prefer for a man. _____

The "look" you prefer for a woman. _____

The city with the most style. _____

Your favourite book or film about fashion. _____

The fashion faux pas you can tolerate most. _____

The fashion faux pas you can tolerate least. _____

What is your present state of mind? _____

Your fashion motto. _____

Your symbol of high fashion. _____

Your favourite fabric. _____

Your favourite colour. _____

The collection you will never forget. _____

The style you most dislike. _____

Your favourite fashion photographer. _____

Your favourite model. _____

Your shoe/shoe designer fetish. _____

Your jewel/jewelry designer fetish. _____

Your favourite fashion accessory. _____

Your ideal bag. _____

The most creative designer. _____

The most timeless designer. _____

Your favourite decade in fashion. _____

Your contemporary muse or inspiration. _____

Your historical muse or icon. _____

The "look" you prefer for a man. _____

The "look" you prefer for a woman. _____

The city with the most style. _____

Your favourite book or film about fashion. _____

The fashion faux pas you can tolerate most. _____

The fashion faux pas you can tolerate least. _____

What is your present state of mind? _____

Your fashion motto. _____

Your symbol of high fashion. _____

Your favourite fabric. _____

Your favourite colour. _____

The collection you will never forget. _____

The style you most dislike. _____

Your favourite fashion photographer. _____

Your favourite model. _____

Your shoe/shoe designer fetish. _____

Your jewel/jewelry designer fetish. _____

Your favourite fashion accessory. _____

Your ideal bag. _____

The most creative designer. _____

The most timeless designer. _____

Your favourite decade in fashion. _____

Your contemporary muse or inspiration. _____

Your historical muse or icon. _____

The "look" you prefer for a man. _____

The "look" you prefer for a woman. _____

The city with the most style. _____

Your favourite book or film about fashion. _____

The fashion faux pas you can tolerate most. _____

The fashion faux pas you can tolerate least. _____

What is your present state of mind? _____

Your fashion motto. _____

Your symbol of high fashion. _____

Your favourite fabric. _____

Your favourite colour. _____

The collection you will never forget. _____

The style you most dislike. _____

Your favourite fashion photographer. _____

Your favourite model. _____

Your shoe/shoe designer fetish. _____

Your jewel/jewelry designer fetish. _____

Your favourite fashion accessory. _____

Your ideal bag. _____

The most creative designer. _____

The most timeless designer. _____

Your favourite decade in fashion. _____

Your contemporary muse or inspiration. _____

Your historical muse or icon. _____

The "look" you prefer for a man. _____

The "look" you prefer for a woman. _____

The city with the most style. _____

Your favourite book or film about fashion. _____

The fashion faux pas you can tolerate most. _____

The fashion faux pas you can tolerate least. _____

What is your present state of mind? _____

Your fashion motto. _____

Your symbol of high fashion. _____

Your favourite fabric. _____

Your favourite colour. _____

The collection you will never forget. _____

The style you most dislike. _____

Your favourite fashion photographer. _____

Your favourite model. _____

Your shoe/shoe designer fetish. _____

Your jewel/jewelry designer fetish. _____

Your favourite fashion accessory. _____

Your ideal bag. _____

The most creative designer. _____

The most timeless designer. _____

Your favourite decade in fashion. _____

Your contemporary muse or inspiration. _____

Your historical muse or icon. _____

The "look" you prefer for a man. _____

The "look" you prefer for a woman. _____

The city with the most style. _____

Your favourite book or film about fashion. _____

The fashion faux pas you can tolerate most. _____

The fashion faux pas you can tolerate least. _____

What is your present state of mind? _____

Your fashion motto. _____

85

Your symbol of high fashion. _____

Your favourite fabric. _____

Your favourite colour. _____

The collection you will never forget. _____

The style you most dislike. _____

Your favourite fashion photographer. _____

Your favourite model. _____

Your shoe/shoe designer fetish. _____

Your jewel/jewelry designer fetish. _____

Your favourite fashion accessory. _____

Your ideal bag. _____

The most creative designer. _____

The most timeless designer. _____

Your favourite decade in fashion. _____

Your contemporary muse or inspiration. _____

Your historical muse or icon. _____

The "look" you prefer for a man. _____

The "look" you prefer for a woman. _____

The city with the most style. _____

Your favourite book or film about fashion. _____

The fashion faux pas you can tolerate most. _____

The fashion faux pas you can tolerate least. _____

What is your present state of mind? _____

Your fashion motto. _____

Your symbol of high fashion. _____

Your favourite fabric. _____

Your favourite colour. _____

The collection you will never forget. _____

The style you most dislike. _____

Your favourite fashion photographer. _____

Your favourite model. _____

Your shoe/shoe designer fetish. _____

Your jewel/jewelry designer fetish. _____

Your favourite fashion accessory. _____

Your ideal bag. _____

The most creative designer. _____

The most timeless designer. _____

Your favourite decade in fashion. _____

Your contemporary muse or inspiration. _____

Your historical muse or icon. _____

The "look" you prefer for a man. _____

The "look" you prefer for a woman. _____

The city with the most style. _____

Your favourite book or film about fashion. _____

The fashion faux pas you can tolerate most. _____

The fashion faux pas you can tolerate least. _____

What is your present state of mind? _____

Your fashion motto. _____

Your symbol of high fashion. _____

Your favourite fabric. _____

Your favourite colour. _____

The collection you will never forget. _____

The style you most dislike. _____

Your favourite fashion photographer. _____

Your favourite model. _____

Your shoe/shoe designer fetish. _____

Your jewel/jewelry designer fetish. _____

Your favourite fashion accessory. _____

Your ideal bag. _____

The most creative designer. _____

The most timeless designer. _____

Your favourite decade in fashion. _____

Your contemporary muse or inspiration. _____

Your historical muse or icon. _____

The "look" you prefer for a man. _____

The "look" you prefer for a woman. _____

The city with the most style. _____

Your favourite book or film about fashion. _____

The fashion faux pas you can tolerate most. _____

The fashion faux pas you can tolerate least. _____

What is your present state of mind? _____

Your fashion motto. _____

Your symbol of high fashion. _____

Your favourite fabric. _____

Your favourite colour. _____

The collection you will never forget. _____

The style you most dislike. _____

Your favourite fashion photographer. _____

Your favourite model. _____

Your shoe/shoe designer fetish. _____

Your jewel/jewelry designer fetish. _____

Your favourite fashion accessory. _____

Your ideal bag. _____

The most creative designer. _____

The most timeless designer. _____

Your favourite decade in fashion. _____

Your contemporary muse or inspiration. _____

Your historical muse or icon. _____

The "look" you prefer for a man. _____

The "look" you prefer for a woman. _____

The city with the most style. _____

Your favourite book or film about fashion. _____

The fashion faux pas you can tolerate most. _____

The fashion faux pas you can tolerate least. _____

What is your present state of mind? _____

Your fashion motto. _____

Your symbol of high fashion.

Your favourite fabric.

Your favourite colour.

The collection you will never forget.

The style you most dislike.

Your favourite fashion photographer.

Your favourite model.

Your shoe/shoe designer fetish.

Your jewel/jewelry designer fetish.

Your favourite fashion accessory.

Your ideal bag.

The most creative designer.

The most timeless designer.

Your favourite decade in fashion.

Your contemporary muse or inspiration.

Your historical muse or icon.

The "look" you prefer for a man.

The "look" you prefer for a woman.

The city with the most style.

Your favourite book or film about fashion.

The fashion faux pas you can tolerate most.

The fashion faux pas you can tolerate least.

What is your present state of mind?

Your fashion motto.

Your symbol of high fashion. _____

Your favourite fabric. _____

Your favourite colour. _____

The collection you will never forget. _____

The style you most dislike. _____

Your favourite fashion photographer. _____

Your favourite model. _____

Your shoe/shoe designer fetish. _____

Your jewel/jewelry designer fetish. _____

Your favourite fashion accessory. _____

Your ideal bag. _____

The most creative designer. _____

The most timeless designer. _____

Your favourite decade in fashion. _____

Your contemporary muse or inspiration. _____

Your historical muse or icon. _____

The "look" you prefer for a man. _____

The "look" you prefer for a woman. _____

The city with the most style. _____

Your favourite book or film about fashion. _____

The fashion faux pas you can tolerate most. _____

The fashion faux pas you can tolerate least. _____

What is your present state of mind? _____

Your fashion motto. _____

Your symbol of high fashion. _____

Your favourite fabric. _____

Your favourite colour. _____

The collection you will never forget. _____

The style you most dislike. _____

Your favourite fashion photographer. _____

Your favourite model. _____

Your shoe/shoe designer fetish. _____

Your jewel/jewelry designer fetish. _____

Your favourite fashion accessory. _____

Your ideal bag. _____

The most creative designer. _____

The most timeless designer. _____

Your favourite decade in fashion. _____

Your contemporary muse or inspiration. _____

Your historical muse or icon. _____

The "look" you prefer for a man. _____

The "look" you prefer for a woman. _____

The city with the most style. _____

Your favourite book or film about fashion. _____

The fashion faux pas you can tolerate most. _____

The fashion faux pas you can tolerate least. _____

What is your present state of mind? _____

Your fashion motto. _____

Your symbol of high fashion. _____

Your favourite fabric. _____

Your favourite colour. _____

The collection you will never forget. _____

The style you most dislike. _____

Your favourite fashion photographer. _____

Your favourite model. _____

Your shoe/shoe designer fetish. _____

Your jewel/jewelry designer fetish. _____

Your favourite fashion accessory. _____

Your ideal bag. _____

The most creative designer. _____

The most timeless designer. _____

Your favourite decade in fashion. _____

Your contemporary muse or inspiration. _____

Your historical muse or icon. _____

The "look" you prefer for a man. _____

The "look" you prefer for a woman. _____

The city with the most style. _____

Your favourite book or film about fashion. _____

The fashion faux pas you can tolerate most. _____

The fashion faux pas you can tolerate least. _____

What is your present state of mind? _____

Your fashion motto. _____

Acknowledgments

The publisher wishes to thank all of the designers who generously answered The Fashion Questionnaire: Thom Browne, Ennio Capasa, Pierre Cardin, Jean-Charles de Castelbajac, Roberto Cavalli, Alber Elbaz, Diane von Furstenberg, John Galliano, Carolina Herrera, Tommy Hilfiger, Donna Karan, Michael Kors, Karl Lagerfeld, Catherine Malandrino, Nicole Miller, Oscar de la Renta, Ralph Rucci, Sonia Rykiel, Olivier Theyskens, Isabel Toledo, and Valentino.

The publisher also wishes to thank: Marie Beaufour, Olivia Berghauer, Olivier Bialobos, Benedetta Bizzi, Hélène Cherifi, Patti Cohen, Billy Daley, Celine Danhier, Eric Delph, Hania Destelle, Caitlin DiStefano, Nicolas Frontière, Larissa Giers, Jean-Pascal Hesse, Miki Higasa, Katelin Jones, Caroline Lebar, Christiano Mancini, Eileen McMaster, Anne Olivieri, Stéphanie Pelian, Alexis Rodriguez, Rosina Rucci, Michelle Yee, and Lucia Zamarron.

Thanks are also due to Gladys Perint Palmer and Francois Berthoud for their illustrations and Michael Specter for his foreword.